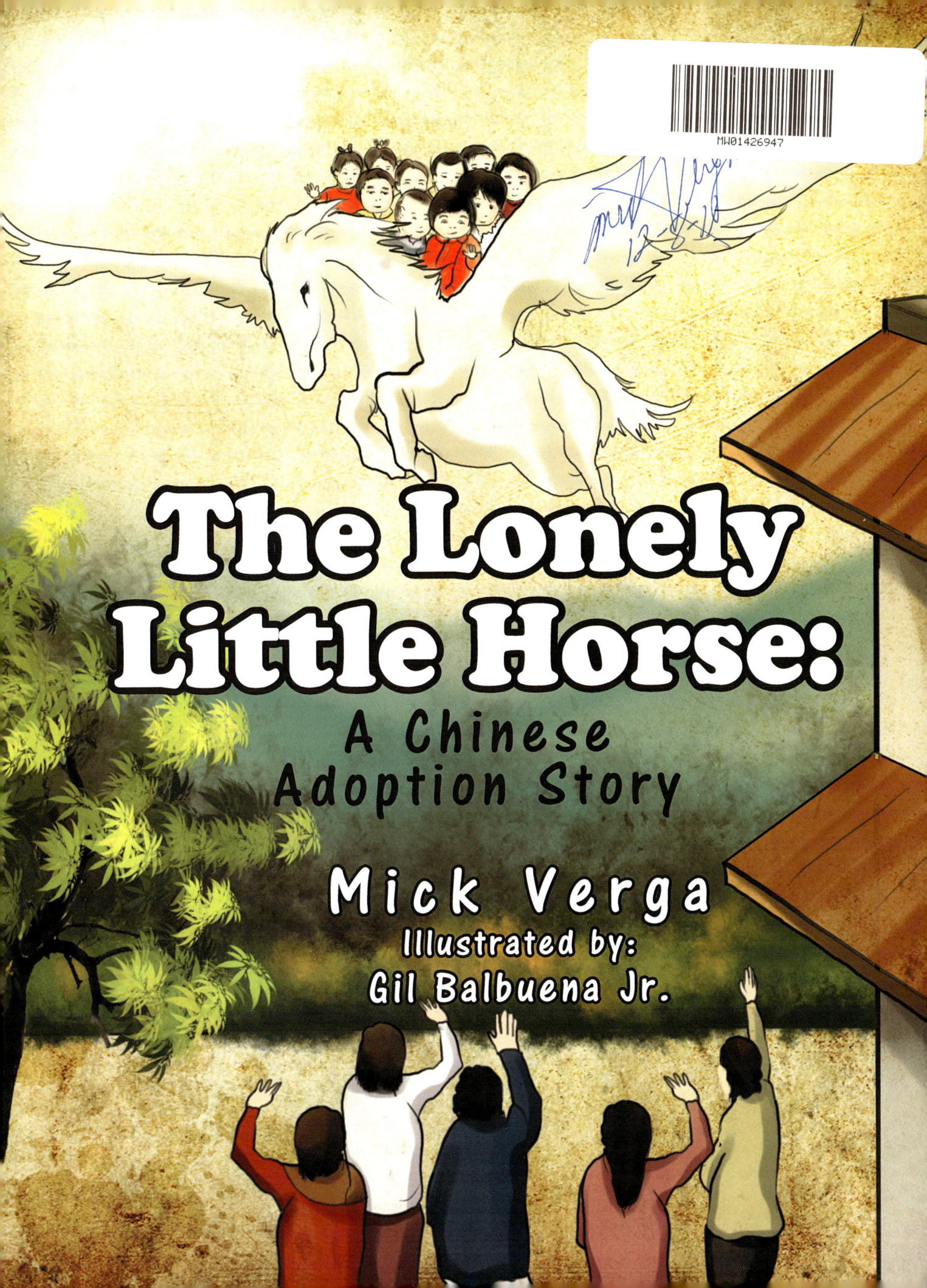

This book is dedicated to my paternal grandfather Captain Dominic Ambrose Verga and my daughter Amanda Yuan Quan Verga.

Both orphans, and God's gifts to our family.

Copyright © 2011 by Mick Verga. 94199-VERG
Library of Congress Control Number: 2011913308
ISBN: Softcover 978-1-4653-4215-7
　　　 Hardcover 978-1-4653-4216-4

All rights reserved. No part of this book may be reproduced or transmitted in any form or by any means, electronic or mechanical, including photocopying, recording, or by any information storage and retrieval system, without permission in writing from the copyright owner.

This is a work of fiction. Names, characters, places and incidents either are the product of the author's imagination or are used fictitiously, and any resemblance to any actual persons, living or dead, events, or locales is entirely coincidental.

This book was printed in the United States of America.

To order additional copies of this book, contact:
Xlibris Corporation
1-888-795-4274
www.Xlibris.com
Orders@Xlibris.com

It was an unseasonably warm night for a Chinese October. Wang Hong had left his windows open to let in the cool night air. Somewhere off in the distance, he thought he heard a cat howling its mournful cry. He turned away from the window to try to go back to sleep. The howl got louder so Wang sat up in bed to try to decide if he should throw a shoe at the cat to make it go away. His wife, Ping Lu, was awakened by his movement.

"What is wrong husband?"

Wang put his finger to his lips and shushed his wife. They both sat there in the darkness listening. The howling had become the unmistakable wail of a crying baby.

Wang and his wife hurried to the window. When they looked outside, they could not believe their eyes. There, right on the front doorstep to their home was a crying baby wrapped in a quilt.

They hurried outside to get the baby to safety before some wild animal came along and harmed it. When they got to the baby, they noticed that she had some blood on her. Wang picked up the note that was pinned to the baby's quilt. It read,

"Please take care of my daughter. I am very poor and have no husband to take care of us. Please be sure that if you cannot provide for her that you find an orphanage that will. Tell my baby that I am sorry and that I will always love her."

Ping Lu and Wang looked at each other. They too were very poor with two children of their own to feed. Without saying a word, Wang knew he would have to go see his brother Dou Ru, who was the director of the local orphanage, at first light. But first they would have to get the baby inside and get her some milk.

Mr. Dou was happy to see his brother Wang at the door, but he was most surprised at the package he was bearing. When Wang explained what had happened, Mr. Dou summoned one of the orphanage nannies. He instructed her to take the baby inside and wash and feed her. After she was finished with that, he wanted her to be clothed in nice warm clothes and cuddled so she could feel some maternal love and affection. Mr. Dou told his brother that this child was a special child and she would be well cared for and receive lots of love.

As Wang got up to leave he asked his brother what he would name the little girl. Mr. Dou explained that all the girls in the orphanage would receive the family name of Chu. It was in honor of their village, Chuzhou and it would give these orphans a family name linking them as sisters forever. Also, all the girls that came to the orphanage this year, The Year of the Horse, would be named Yen. Each girl would have a special middle name. This girl would be called Chen which means "spring water." It was hoped she would grow up to be like spring water, pure and sweet.

Life at the orphanage was hard for the baby, now called ChenChen by the nannies. She and her sisters were always very cold because the building had no heat and very little food. The babies slept two and three to a crib. They wore homemade flannel clothes that were so puffy to keep warm that they looked like astronauts. ChenChen was the tiniest child and did not get to have much time on the floor with the other children so she would not get hurt. She was either in a walker or left in her crib until she cried so hard the nannies had to pick her up and hold her. ChenChen loved to be held and after awhile all the nannies loved to hold her all the time. She was the most beautiful baby they had ever seen. She would sit on her nannies lap, just looking around surveying her sisters. One nanny said ChenChen reminded her of a lonely little horse, waiting to be accepted into the herd.

One day, about six months later, there was much commotion in the big room. The nannies had gathered up the ten oldest sisters, got them dressed in new clothes, and brought them out to a waiting white van. They never came back.

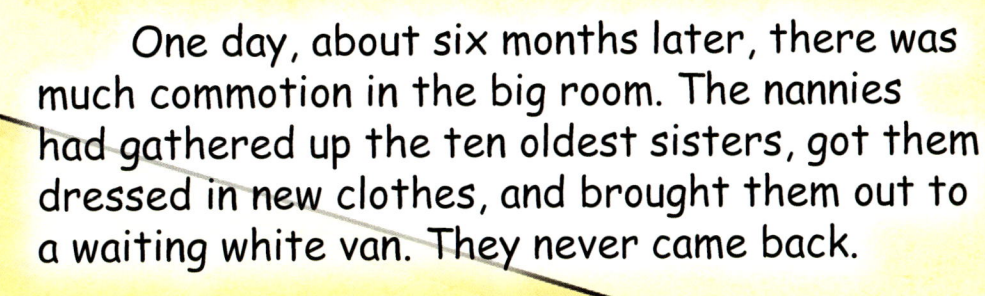

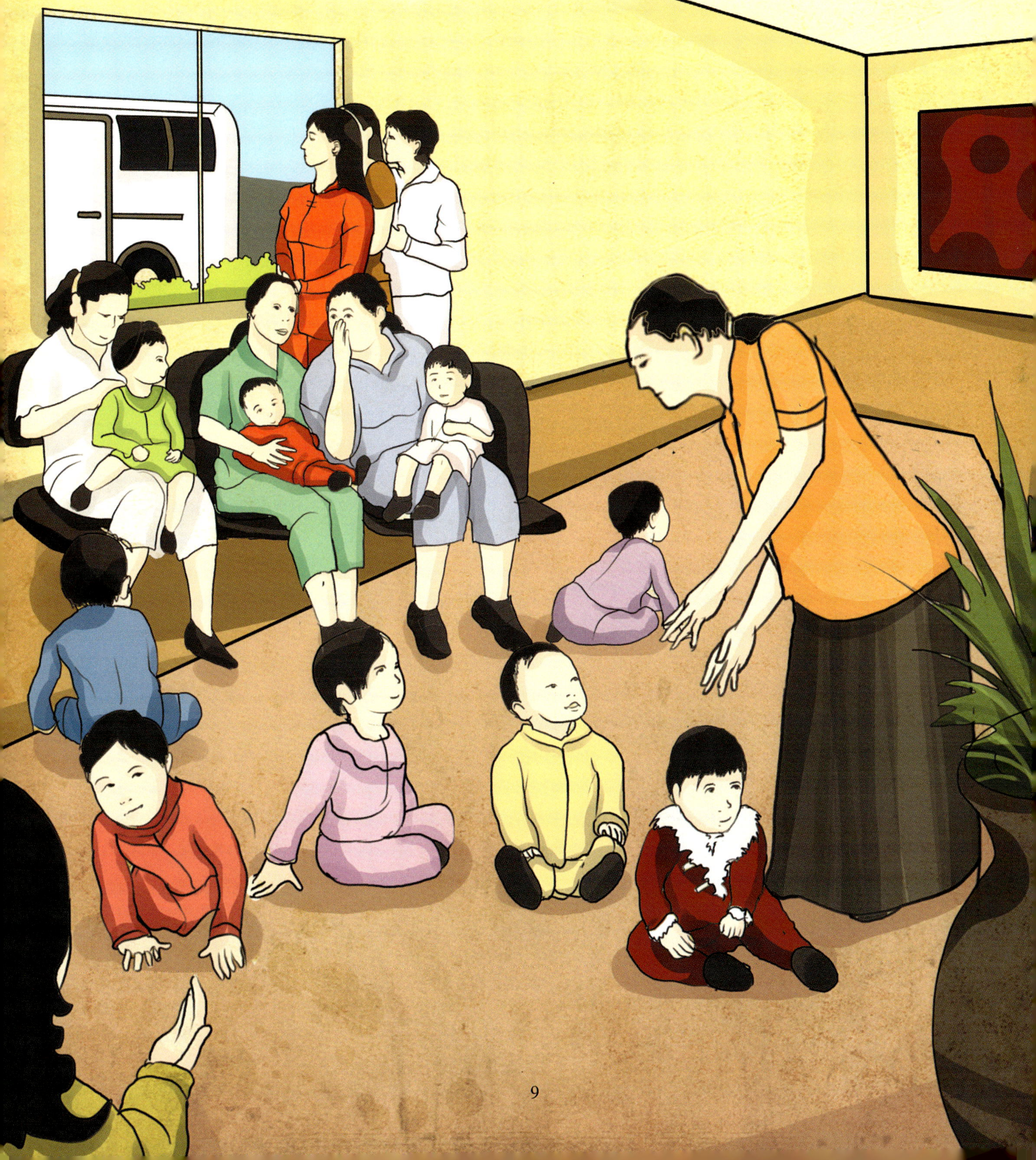

Now, very few people outside of China know this little secret. Chinese babies have special powers that let them communicate with each other in grown up conversation. To an adult it might sound like "googoogaagaa" but to Chinese babies, especially ones born in The Year of the Horse, they can converse like a grown up.

As the girls sat in the big room, a few weeks after the others left, the oldest sister, DanDan, told the girls that the older sisters had been adopted. ChenChen asked if that meant that they had been eaten by a giant dragon.

"No" said MinMin, ChenChen's crib mate along with DanDan. "It means a Mama and Baba had come for each girl and brought them home to make a family."

ChenChen was very excited. She wanted to be adopted and have a family too. She would pray hard to Buddha every day so that she and her little horse sisters would soon have a new family.

ChenChen and her sisters had grown into beautiful little girls, but ChenChen had a beauty that radiated. She was by far the favorite of the nannies. They knew that as happy as they would be for ChenChen to have a family, they would be very sad when she left to join her new family.

When ChenChen was just past a year old she was lying in her crib with MinMin and DanDan. DanDan said she heard the nannies talking about some people coming from a far away place called America. They would be here in a few months to adopt some of the children from the orphanage.

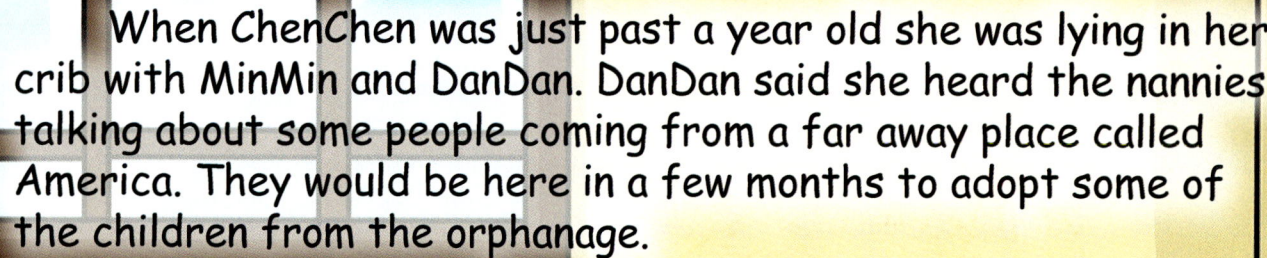

The girls were very excited but at the same time, very sad. They would be leaving their nannies who had been like mamas to them, but worst of all, they would be leaving each other. They decided to make a pact. They would make their mama and baba take them away once a year for a weekend and have a reunion. Now, all they had to do was wait and hope the entire horse sisters went together.

Nearly six months had gone by since the news of the visitors impending arrival. Then one weekend, ChenChen noticed the nannies seemed sad. They had tears in their eyes each time they held or fed the girls. Then one day, Mr. Dou gathered all ten sisters in the big room. The nannies were opening packages of new clothes and starting to put them on all the sisters. The last time something happened like this was... today must be the day! When ChenChen's nanny picked her up, ChenChen could see a white van outside the window. Today the sisters were going to get their families! The nannies hurriedly dressed the children for the long drive to Hefei, the capital of Anhui. The new families were waiting for the children at a Holiday Inn. The children were loaded in the van and off they went.

Inside a large conference room, the nannies sat holding the children. Men with stern faces were sitting at long table filled with paperwork. It was a very chaotic scene but at the same time, very controlled. Mr. Dou looked at the guide for the adoptive parents and told her that they were ready. The guide went to each room and told the excited parents to be in the conference room in ten minutes. The children were waiting for them.

Ten minutes later, a chorus of crying babies erupted. The babies had only seen one man, Mr. Dou, and black haired Asian eyed woman during their short lives. Now all these people with round eyes and all different color hair were holding the children and the children were letting their displeasure be known. All ChenChen's sisters were now with their new families. QuiQui, YinYin, YeYe, YuanYuan, DanDan, MinMin, KeKe, HanHan, and ZhouZhou were being held by strange looking people and did not seem to be very happy.

Mr. Dou was still holding ChenChen who quietly looked around at this confusion. She wondered if they had forgotten to find her a family. Suddenly, the guide came over to Mr. Dou and took ChenChen from his arms. Mr. Dou put his head in his hands and began to quietly weep. This was a special child to him, brought to him by his brother and he held a deep love in his heart for her. Mr. Dou looked up just in time to see the guide handing ChenChen to a beautiful Chinese woman who was with a very big American man with a shaved head who reminded Mr. Dou of Buddha. This made Mr. Dou smile.
He knew ChenChen's prayers to Buddha were answered.

He heard the guide say "ChenChen, this is your mama and baba" and then walk away.

The woman holding ChenChen spoke to her in Chinese. "ChenChen, I am your mama and this is your baba. We love you."

The man spoke to ChenChen in a language she had never heard before but she probably would not have understood him anyway because he was crying. ChenChen felt very comfortable being held by her new mama and baba. She was the only sister that did not cry.

Later, in her new room with her new mama and baba, ChenChen tried to figure out what was going on. Her new mama had undressed her and was examining her. When her mama was through examining her, she picked her up and brought her to another room. It had a large container filled with water. ChenChen had never seen one of these before. Her mama called it a bathtub and put ChenChen in it. Now she screamed like her sisters! She had only sat in a wash basin before and this was scaring her. Her mama got in the tub with her and sang to her in Chinese and ChenChen stopped crying.

The next day, the group traveled back to the orphanage to see where their children had begun their lives.

As they walked through the door all the nannies shouted, "ChenChen, ChenChen!"

They ran up to ChenChen's new mama and began to talk to her in Chinese. It wasn't often that they got to talk to adoptive parents in their native language. They took ChenChen in their arms and hugged and kissed her as if they had not seen her in many years. They told her mama about all her likes and dislikes. They told mama how ChenChen loved to be held and how she enjoyed looking at her self in the mirror. The nannies were very happy ChenChen had a new family with a nice mama and baba. They were especially happy that her new mama was Chinese and would teach ChenChen the language and culture of the land that she had come from. They were also happy to hear that DanDan had been adopted by someone from the same city as ChenChen. That meant that they would grow up together, keeping that sister bond from Chuzhou.

Before the group returned to the hotel, ChenChen's mama and baba asked if they could see the crib she slept in. They put her in the crib to take a picture but she did not want to be in there. She was afraid she was going to have to stay. She started crying so it was one quick picture and out of the crib. She held on to her mama so tight as if to say, take me with you, please don't leave me here.

As they left the orphanage, the nannies tears were tears of joy this time. They knew ChenChen had found the family she wanted and ChenChen knew it too. As ChenChen got on the bus with her mama and baba, her nanny said she no longer looked like the lonely little horse as she and her sisters galloped off to their new lives with their new families in America.